Opening Doors: Roe v Wade

Opening Doors: Roe v Wade

Linda Robertson Bourgeois, Ph.D.

Published by MRR Publishers, 2021.

While every precaution has been taken in the preparation of this book, the publisher assumes no responsibility for errors or omissions, or for damages resulting from the use of the information contained herein.

OPENING DOORS: ROE V WADE

First edition. August 15, 2021.

ISBN: 979-8201593636

Written by Linda Robertson Bourgeois, Ph.D..

Table of Contents

Opening Doors: Roe v Wade
Public Policy
Linda Robertson Bourgeois, Ph.D.

Dedication

For all the young ladies who walked
through the doors of The Pink Building

Foreword

———

The world has evolved during my professional career and so have our social conventions. I graduated from the Air Force Academy in 1968 and then went to medical school. In 1973 following a Supreme Court decision, female Air Force members were for the first time allowed to have adopted children (or their own children) occupy family housing on base and given all the same privileges as children of male members. Then in 1975 pregnant female members had a choice to be discharged or remain in service if they were pregnant or decided to adopt. In 1976 the WAF (Women's Air Force) was terminated, and women were in the regular Air Force and the first women were selected for pilot school and for admission to the Air Force Academy. The world had changed indeed. No longer were pregnant Air Force members discharged from service.

Pregnancies have a 25% spontaneous miscarriage rate of which the mother will recognize 10-15%. Worldwide, elective abortions are estimated to account for 25% of pregnancies with fifty-six million abortions per year in 2010-2020. The rate is the same in countries where the procedure is legal or illegal. Many concerned citizens know that a legal abortion is much safer than an illegal one and is also much cheaper. The decision of a mother to have an abortion is a very personal one and society must be respectful of personal liberty. The responsibility of society to respect the right of the unborn fetus over the mother's right is another issue which brings in ethical issues which require respect as well. Citizens who feel strongly about this justly refuse that their tax dollars are used to kill fetuses. It is a political situation fraught with controversy that our Republic must resolve to suture the wounds of our civil society while protecting the liberty of voting citizens.

LINDA ROBERTSON BOURGEOIS, PH.D.

This review of the legal history of abortion law in the United States is timely. We need to pause and slowly come to consensus on this issue. The States will each have a different way of resolving this. The constitution is to protect life, liberty, and the pursuit of happiness. Abortion puts this all-in conflict. Respecting this reality on the part of all parties of these disagreements perhaps will help bring a resolution for us all.

As a physician, you are there to help the patient. They often refuse to stop smoking, drinking alcohol, or abusing drugs, but you still must care for them in any case. Desperate pregnant women can be suicidal and pressures to pursue a career, or a disrupted relationship, or health and mental health issues confound decision making. Providing a safe abortion to women who have made their decision about an abortion is a positive public good for many. A country which defends this liberty deserves citizen support as well as respect for those dissenting.

Warren D. Everett, M.D.

Preface

At 17 she was pregnant. I did not know what she would do and never found out.

My life went on without any thought about her and what she might be feeling or having to deal with because of the situation. After graduating from college, my teaching career started and years later another brilliant young lady, who was graduating, gave up her scholarships and immediately departed to spend time away from home, to visit with her grandmother in another state.

This is one of the ways young girls dealt with unwanted pregnancies back then.

A student at Calhoun Community College asked for my vita' and I gave it to her without asking why. She gave it to the Vice President of the Women's Community Health Center. They were hiring for a new administrator. Drinking coffee while preparing for class one morning, I received a phone call asking me to come in for an interview. I asked the lady who she was and what position I was interviewing for because I had not applied for a position. The lady laughed and said "You do not know who I am." And I said "No." After she explained I said I would come to the hotel before class to speak with her. The interview was delightful and as I left, we both said we would keep in touch. The next day I received another phone call from the same lady asking me to come back in and I told her I would however, it would have to be after class but would swing by the hotel on my way home. I did not know the field had narrowed to two. During this meeting, the Vice President stated she thought we should be co-directors and I said, "No." I thought the other person, who worked at the clinic, was more qualified. I also stated that two people could not run a clinic successfully as one voice. The next day the position was mine.

The first day I walked through the line of protestors yelling at me. How strange this felt from entering the halls of academia where the only yelling was one of greeting not that I was the devil. Two volunteers walked me in and unbeknownst to me they took bets on how long I would stay. I was a small person and thin. I never gave up on hard positions.

The first day was the most difficult. I watched every position and person perform their job and it was not until I saw the first abortion performed that I became weak; however, with jaw set I continued, and the day ended. I walked to my car independently. Protestors only protest while the patients are arriving.

As I mulled things over in my mind that night, I thought that just maybe there were things we could do different. Would they be better? Only time would tell. I had confidence in the professionally qualified staff and with their help in educating me we could do this together. My dream was to have a model clinic for all the naysayers to see. Small steps would bring us to our goal.

With willing hands, we started first with the cleanup of the building. We first cleaned out about two tons of paper or junk; repainted the entire building; rewrote every protocol; retrained every person; hung lace curtains on all windows; ordered new gowns; and one staff member made new lap covers; the building was clean from top to bottom.

Sometimes I wonder how I learned it all but if my mother could go back to school at 59 and get her nursing degree and go on to become a surgical nurse then I would be the best Administrator ever in the eyes of my deceased mom. As a previous counselor at the Mental Health Center and having taught psychology at both the University and Community

College level, I thought I had the mental capacity to learn every position and perform every job. If I were going to ask someone else to do a job, then I must be willing to do that job as well. I must learn it better than they. Therefore, I learned.

Even though each staff member knew their job well, I wanted to make sure they also knew every young lady who came to our clinic was there on the worst day of her life. Sympathy and tough love must be a part of our discussion. The discussion opener made the process easy. If it were your daughter, what would you have us do?

We also taught birth control methods including the right to say "No." The most difficult clients were the repeat clients. Abortion, in our opinion, was not a method of birth control.

Time passed and the building had a new feel to it. One could walk in and know that all of us cared not only for them but also for each other. We were a family. We had each other's back. All of us were extremely proud of what we had accomplished as a team. We held an open house for the public to see the new/old building. The yard was lovely. The entire building was very pretty...as pretty as any doctor's office.

We had no secrets. During the tour of the building, at every station a person was there to explain what we did before the young lady had the abortion.

I manned the counseling station. The decision to have an abortion is a difficult permanent decision. They had 24 hours to decide if this were something they could live with for the rest of their lives, if not then walk away.

As a licensed Alabama Abortion clinic, we were the best. The staff stayed with me for 12 years. Each person I hired I explained the possibility of not ever going home again; this was the underlying principle. I think we all believed and trusted that a higher power knew our hearts and how we conducted our job and would protect us.

Three examples of patients one could find in any clinic in any state:

A child thirteen, mentally retarded with the mind of a 2-year-old brought her doll with her. Her family had tried to get permission for sterilization, but failed. The system had failed.

A young lady taken and held, without her consent, raped by multiple men for a week. For the case to stand up in court, chain of custody followed, therefore the police remained in the room during the abortion and accepted the fetus directly from the doctor. Tears flowed without shame from everyone...

A couple came in with a dead child in utero. It was a wanted child, and they were sad and angry. Here they were standing in an abortion clinic aborting a dead child watching others who were there aborting an unwanted fetus. It seemed unusually cruel to them. Her doctor sent her for the procedure.

To explain the difference between a "child" and a "fetus" a fetus becomes a child at week twenty-two when the brain begins to function. Without a brain, there is no pain or thought.

> *"This illustrates the agony, yet empathy of the situation, as well as the tragedy of the situation." Warren Everett, MD*

Speaking of doctors, the majority of ob/gyns in cities and towns across our nation perform abortions for their patients. Most do not know this. Our clinic also helped the hospitals by lending our equipment, when necessary.

Confidentiality was an absolute. Break it and you were immediately terminated. Only once did this happen to my knowledge. With deep sorrow, I terminated her. She had not realized how it happened until I explained to her what happened. It was not her intention to break confidentiality.

The world has changed. Do we change because morals and values have changed? Has social media made us smarter or dumber? Does it matter what we the people believe any more? Where is integrity and honesty? Questions. No answers.

I changed but not because the world changed. I changed because my world changed. Maybe that is part of the answer. There are worlds within worlds and our lives touch briefly as we move through this Universe for our short time on life's stage.

Has my position changed now I am eighty-three? No. I am an Independent leaning conservative. My body is mine and the government has no right to tell me what I can and cannot do. We all have a choice. If you remember nothing else from this short paper, remember you have a Choice. Exercise that choice.

Acknowledgements

It would be impossible to acknowledge all those who helped me become the person who could author this paper. There were doctors, nurses, staff, and friends who believed in what I was doing...that is, going to work every day to provide a "safe" place for women to come and discuss or exercise their right to choose. I had always championed different causes, and this became my last and greatest cause.

For all those who gave their lives to this cause, thank you.

For all those who risk their lives every day to preserve the right of women to choose, thank you.

For all the Clinic Staff who came and stayed or came and left at Women's Community Health Center, thank you. You were the best!

And, to all the patients who were brave enough to walk through our doors for whatever reason, thank you for trusting us.

Isaiah 10: 1-3

"Woe to those who decree iniquitous decrees, And the writers who keep writing oppression, to turn aside the needy from justice and to rob the poor of my people of their right, that widows may be their spoil, and that they may make the fatherless their prey! What will you do on the day of punishment, in the storm which will come from afar? To whom will you flee for help, and where will you leave your wealth?"

Introduction

Roe v. Wade was the second time in American history that the Supreme Court invoked "substantive due process" to deny American citizens authority to protect the basic rights of an entire class of human beings. The first time was the 1857 Court decision in *Dred Scott v. Sandford* (60 U. S. 393, 1857). The Court held that the Missouri Compromise of 1820, prohibiting slavery in the northern portion of the Louisiana Territories, constitutionally could not be applied to those persons who brought their slaves into free territory. The Court asserted that such a prohibition "could hardly be dignified with the name of due process" (Id at 450). The people tried to resolve, both peacefully and politically, this great moral issue, however, Chief Justice Taney, and his concurring colleagues, thought they were resolving the issue of slavery for the last time. This only made matters worse. Four years later the Civil War erupted. Like *Dred Scott*, Roe has been the great divisive issue of this age (Whelan, 2000).

Historical Background

Abortions can be traced back over four thousand years. However, the law, with respect to abortion in mid-19th century America, followed existing common law of England, which had banned all abortions in 1803, followed by Africa, Asia, and Latin America (Olasky, 1992; Milbauer, 1983. Rosen, 1954).

Banned or restricted by many religions, abortion was not considered illegal until after this time. "In October 1869, Pope Pius IX condemned abortion and reminded Catholics of the church's long-standing sanctions against it" (Milbauer, 1983). Before the mid-19th century nobody really concerned themselves with the issue until after quickening unless it was proven to be a male child (Milbauer, 1983).

In early American history, there were three groups of women having abortions: those who had been seduced, prostitutes, and some specific groups among the married (Olasky, 1992). Advertisements for abortifacients appeared regularly across the country. Anna Lohman, known as Madame Restell, along with her husband, openly marketed abortifacients primarily in New England from 1841 to 1878 (Olasky, 1992; Milbauer, 1983; Rosen, 1954). Anthony Comstock, Special Agent of the Post Office Department, was appointed to enforce the 1873 law that banned use of the nation's mails to circulate obscene materials. This act included contraceptive information and devices on its forbidden list. Comstock and his supporters went undercover to search out those who were engaged in the abortion business. This sent abortionist into hiding for a while. Three years later, Madame Restell was convicted for being an abortionist and committed suicide. New York rejoiced that "Among notable cases disposed of the past year is that of the closing effectually of the gilded hall of death on Fifth Avenue, kept by Ann Lohman, better known as Madame Restell" (Olasky, 1992). Comstock did not persevere in the abortion battle after this, turning his attention to other areas. Abortionist advertising appeared once more not only in New York but also across the United States (Olasky, 1992).

By the time of the Civil War, an influential anti-abortion movement began to affect legislation by inducing states to add to or revise their statutes to prohibit abortion at all stages of gestation except for therapeutic abortions which were encouraged for certain ethnic populations: Chinese, Germans, Irish, Italians and Black people because American meant white, Anglo- Saxon Protestant (Milbauer, 1983).

In 1912, Margaret Sanger, a district nurse in the slum areas of New York, was incensed because of the large amount of death and invalidism which she saw resulting from too frequent childbearing. At much personal sacrifice, after the preventable death following a criminal abortion of a mother of several children, she brought together several people who were as disturbed about the situation as she was and the idea of the control of the number of births as well as the length of time between births emerged. "The idea of the control of the number of births, and even of the length of time between births, was not new—ancient history contains many references to it—but to many Americans fifty years ago this seemed a radical and even immoral concept" (Rosen, 1954). Ms. Sanger and her followers formed a national organization, The American Birth Control League, Inc. This organization, in 1941, became Planned Parenthood Federation of America, Inc. (Rosen, 1954).

Development And Status of The Law Prior To 1973

By 1910, every state had anti-abortion laws, except Kentucky; forty-nine states and the District of Columbia classified the crime of abortion as a felony. The states varied in their exceptions for therapeutic abortions. Forty- two states permitted abortions only to save the life of the woman. Three states allowed abortions that were not "unlawfully performed." Other states allowed abortion to save a woman from "serious permanent bodily injury" or her "life and health." This represents the high-water mark in restrictive abortion laws in the United States (Mohr, 1978).

Changing attitudes began to prevail around 1965 when the Supreme Court, in *Griswold v Connecticut* (1965), found that a state statute making it a crime to use birth control violated married couples' right to privacy and seven years later applied this right to single people as well in *Eisenstadt v Baird* (1972).

However, the legalization of abortion began in Mississippi in 1966, when a law permitting abortion in cases of rape was passed (Merz, 2007). Alabama, Colorado, New Mexico, and Massachusetts were the first to permit abortion when a woman's physical or mental health was in jeopardy (Stateline.org). Colorado and California, in 1967, passed abortion reform legislation based on the Model Penal Code developed by the American Law Institute in 1962. This legislation would allow abortions when childbirth posed grave danger to the physical or mental health of a woman, when there was high likelihood of fetal abnormality, or when pregnancy resulted from rape or incest. By 1972, Arkansas, Delaware, Florida, Georgia, Kansas, Maryland, New

Mexico, North Carolina, Oregon, South Carolina, and Virginia had followed (Stateline.org). By the end of 1970, four states (Alaska, Hawaii, New York, and Washington) had repealed criminal penalties for abortions performed by a licensed physician and early in pregnancy subject only to stated procedural and health requirements. However, most states failed to loosen their laws, leaving women, including victims of rape and incest, few legal options. (Stateline.org).

In 1971, the first U. S. Supreme Court decision dealing specifically with abortion was rendered in *United States v. Vuitch*. The *Vuitch* decision essentially expanded the availability of abortions under the D. C. law's provision allowing abortions where "necessary for the preservation of the mother's...health" (*United States v. Vuitch*, 1971).

Roe V. Wade

In 1973, there were two cases decided by the Supreme Court which in effect not only legalized abortion but also constitutionalized abortions for any reason through the 24th week of pregnancy. Those historic cases were *Roe v Wade* and its companion case *Doe v Bolton*. Before *Roe* and *Doe*, the American people had the constitutional authority, through their state legislatures, to make abortion policy in their respective states. These two decisive decisions deprived the American people of this authority only allowing individual states to enact laws restricting abortion after viability, except in cases when abortion is necessary to preserve the life and health of the woman (*Merz & McGee, 2007*).

In Roe v Wade, 410 U. S. 113 (1973), the Court addressed the constitutionality of a Texas statue, "typical of those that have been in effect in many States for approximately a century," that made abortion a crime except where "procured or attempted by medical advice for the purpose of saving the life of the mother" (Id at 116, 118). The seven-Justice majority, in an opinion by Justice Blackmun, ruled that the Texas statute violated the Due Process Clause of the Fourteenth Amendment (which provides that no state shall "deprive any person of life, liberty, or property, with due process of law"). The Court ruled that the Due Process Clause requires an abortion regime that comports with these requirements that the Court composed:

> a) For the stage prior to approximately the end of the first trimester, the abortion decision and its effectuation must be left to the medical judgment of the pregnant woman's attending physician.

b) For the stage subsequent to approximately the end of the first trimester, the State, in promoting its interest in the health of the mother, may, if it chooses, regulate the abortion procedure in ways that are reasonably related to maternal health.

c) For the stage subsequent to viability, the State in promoting its interest in the potentiality of human life may, if it chooses, regulate, and even proscribe, abortion except where it is necessary, in appropriate medical judgment, for the preservation of the life or health of the mother" (Id. At 164-165).

The same day that the Court decided Roe, it rendered its decision in *Doe v Bolton*, 410 U. S. 179 (1973). According to the Court, *Roe* and *Doe* "are to be read together" (*Roe* 410 U. S. at 165). Doe presented the question whether Georgia's abortion legislation, patterned on the American Law Institute's model legislation, was constitutional (410 U. S. at 181-182). The Georgia statute provided that an abortion shall not be criminal when performed by a physician "based upon his best clinical judgment that an abortion is necessary because (a) continuation of the pregnancy would endanger the life of the pregnant woman or (b) would seriously and permanently injure her health" (Id at 183). While upholding this provision against a challenge that it was unconstitutionally vague, Blackmun's majority opinion determined that the "medical judgment (as to health) may be exercised in the light of all factors – physical, emotional, psychological, familial, and the woman's age – relevant to the wellbeing of the patient.

All these factors may relate to health. This allows the attending physician the room he needs to make his best medical judgment" (Id. at 192). The authority that Roe purports to confer on states to "regulate, and even proscribe, abortion" after viability is subject to the loophole of Doe's health exception (*Women's Medical Professional Corp. v Voinovich*, 130 F. 3d 187, 209 (6th Cir. 1997). The practical meaning then of this loophole would appear to be that an abortion could be performed at the discretion of the abortionist and would swallow any general post-viability prohibition.

Other key issues began to emerge, i.e., rights of minors to have an abortion was decided by the Supreme Court in 1976 in *Planned Parenthood of Central Missouri v. Danforth* and three years later the Court enacted further standards that required either parental consent or judicial bypass for pregnant girls under the age of eighteen. In 1977, the Supreme Court addressed the issue of federal funds being used for abortions (*The 1977 Trilogy – Restrictions on Public Funding of Nontherapeutic or Elective Abortions*) limiting the use of Medicaid funds for payment of elective abortions; and, in 1980, the Court restricted Medicaid funds to be paid only in cases where an abortion is necessary to preserve the woman's life (*Harris v McRae*, 448 U. S. 297, 1980). While Supreme Court Decisions since 1973 – including *Harris v. McRae* and *Webster v. Reproductive Health Services*, 492 U. S. 490, 1989 – have reduced federal spending for abortions, thereby limiting free services for poor women and minors, the basic premise of *Roe v. Wade* was upheld in 1992 in *Planned Parenthood of Southeastern Pennsylvania v Casey*, 505 U. S. 833 (1992) (*Women's Rights on Trial*, 1997).

Program Development and Implementation

P ublic Policies are seldom self-executing (Bond, Johnson, and Texas A. & M. University, 1982). The impact of a policy is likely to vary because those who implement a policy are subject to political pressures that are totally different from those who formulate the policy (Bond, et. al., 1982). As with other civil liberty policies, whether individuals can exercise their rights depends on actions and organizations that implement the policy. In the *Roe v Wade* (1973) case the primary implementers of the policy were private clinics and hospitals. Even though abortion was legalized, many women lack access because of restrictive legislation which especially burdens poor and young women, an inability to pay, the uneven geographic concentration of services, and the shortage of providers (Guttmacher, 2000).

The Supreme Court decisions in *Roe* and *Doe* did not address several abortion-related issues. In seeking to restrict the scope of the Court's rulings, states had to address the issues of informed consent, spousal consent, parental consent, and reporting requirements as well as what abortion procedures may be required or prohibited by statute. The Court did not resolve the question of when life begins, defining it in legal terms, yet noting that there was a divergence of thinking, as the point at which the fetus is potentially able to live outside the womb, although the fetus may require artificial aid (Roe, 410 U. S. at 160).

Each individual state developed their respective programs through rules and regulations set forth by the Public Health Department in a separate division called Abortion Service Providers. Public funding was limited to non-existent. Public institutions were inaccessible to most women therefore, after the *Roe v. Wade* ruling, private clinics were established with the first two chains being opened by two Jewish businesspeople, Lipton and Leight. Planned Parenthood provided healthcare services for women but did not provide abortions until the late 1990's in most states. No standardized rules and regulations were issued from the National/Federal level providing opportunity for opponents within the state governments to set prohibitive rules and regulations for independent clinics to follow. The Rules and Regulations were more restrictive compared to the rules for physicians' offices and other outpatient clinics. Not only were there rules and regulations set forth by the State Departments of Health but also there were Occupational Safety and Health Association rules to be followed; Nursing Standards to be put in place; Drug Enforcement Administration rules to be followed; Physicians Rules and Medical Examiner Rules for Physicians, Vital Statistics rules; Fire and Health Code rules ... a plethora of rules and regulations all governing abortion service providers. This set the stage for more litigation to clarify the issues. So, there really was no implementation phase...one could say there was and is only the litigation phase.

The Supreme Court did not stipulate that there would be fiscal support designated for *Roe v Wade*. A few states had funds available for abortions; Medicaid paid for abortions to preserve a woman's life but for the most part each patient was responsible for paying for the service before the procedure was performed. Insurance companies very rarely paid for an abortion unless it could be deemed as therapeutic. Implementation became a hodge-podge of state rules and regulations. The lack of guidance...the non-implementation of *Roe v Wade* there were both positive and negative actions. The positives would be Women could choose where to obtain services if they had the necessary funds. Clinics mandated confidentiality of the patient's identity whereas if government funds were used several layers of persons might know what was happening. Physicians could provide services, without fear of reprisal, in their offices and deem those procedures as therapeutic to the insurance companies.

Some of the negative consequences: unequal access to services; poor women were forced to have children they could not care for appropriately; Medicaid funding increased for children to unwed mothers; more tax dollars were appropriated for the care of these illegitimate children; crime increased overcrowding jails.

Program Evaluation

———

Roe v *Wade* was only the beginning. The Supreme Court Justices have repeatedly heard cases to clarify the intent of Roe. There have been thirty or more cases to date preserving the right to choose but at the same time narrowing the intent of the law opening the door even further to political and religious debate over the legality of *Roe*.

It is even more difficult to evaluate a policy that was never implemented. Justice Harry A. Blackmun wrote the *Roe v Wade* ruling and declared that the guarantee of liberty in the 14th Amendment to the U. S. Constitution extends a right to privacy "broad enough to encompass a woman's decision whether or not to terminate her pregnancy" (*Roe v Wade,* 1973). This ruling made abortion legal in all states. Blackmun also wrote that "this right is not unqualified and must be considered against important state interests in regulation" (Roe v Wade, 1973). So, this exception by Blackmun gave some leverage to those opposing abortions sparking debates that have polarized the American political atmosphere like no other issue. Polls have shown that most Americans oppose abortion but do not oppose a woman's right to choose. This ruling by the Supreme Court sparked violence against women, their families, clinic workers and medical doctors beginning and continuing from then until now. The latest issue is whether the Court will grant the fetus legal "personhood" giving it the same rights as children and adults. If this should happen then the door would be open for the Court to overturn the rights guaranteed by *Roe v Wade*. Abortions would still be performed whether legal or illegal because the reversal of Roe would restore to the people of the States their constitutional authority to establish...or to revise over time...the abortion laws and policies for their respective states.

As Justice Scalia suggested in his dissent in Casey, Chief Justice Taney believed that his Dred Scott opinion would resolve, finally, the slavery question. But Scalia continued:

> a) It is no more realistic for us in this case, than it was for him in that, to think that an issue of the sort they both involved – an issue involving life and death, freedom and subjugation – can be 'speedily and finally settled' by the Supreme Court, as President James Buchanan in his inaugural address said the issue of slavery in the territories would be...Quite to the contrary, by foreclosing all democratic outlet for the deep passions this issue arouses, by banishing the issue from the political forum that gives all participants, even the losers, the satisfaction of a fair hearing and an honest fight, by continuing the imposition of a rigid national rule instead of allowing for regional differences, the Court merely prolongs and intensifies the anguish.

> b) We should get out of this area, where we have no right to be, and where we do neither ourselves nor the country any good by remaining." 505 U. S. at 1002.

The similarity or parallel between the Dred Scott decision and the Court's abortion decision is this: The abolitionists who wanted to end human slavery fought against the Dred Scott decision. Those who want women to be enslaved by laws requiring childbirth if a woman is impregnated by rape, incest, failure of contraception, etc. are fighting against the Supreme Court decision legalizing abortion. The abolitionists fought for the freedom and right of self-determination of black slaves. The pro-choice movement fights for the right of women legally to determine their own destiny and to control their bodies. Dred Scott symbolized the inequality of black slaves with free whites and free blacks. The problem today is that "right to life" political and religious leaders want to take millions of women and make them as a class not only unequal to men but also subordinate to the fetuses they carry in their wombs (Swomley, 1997).

References

Abortion Law Homepage Bond, J. R. & Johnson, C. A. Implementing a Permissive Policy:

Hospital Abortion Services after *Roe v Wade. American Journal of Political Science*, Vol. 26. No. 1 (Feb. 1982). Pp. 1-24.

Doe v Bolton, 410 U. S. 179 (1973).

Dred Scott v. Sanford, 60 U. S. 393, (1857).

Eisenstadt v. Baird, 405 U. S. 438 (1972).

http://www.ppnep.org/tieline.htm[1]   http://www.npr.org/news/specials/roev-wade/timeline.html

Griswold v. Connecticut, 381 U. S. 479 (1965).

Harris v. McRae, 448 U. S. 297, (1980).

Merz, J. F. & McGee, G. (2007). Bioethics. University of Pennsylvania.

Milbauer, B. (1983). The Law Giveth: Legal Aspects of the Abortion Controversy. Athenaeum: New York.

Mohr, J. C. (1978). Abortion in America: The Origins and Evolution of National Policy, 1800-1900. New York: Oxford University Press.

Olasky, M. (1992). Abortion Rites: A Social History of Abortion in America. Illinois: Crossway Books.

Planned Parenthood v. Casey, 505 U. S. 833 (1992).

---

1. http://www.ppnep.org/tieline.htm%20

"Revisiting Public Funding of Abortion for Poor women," The Guttmacher Report on Public Policy, April 2000.

Rosen, H. (Ed.) (1954). Therapeutic Abortion: Medical, Psychiatric, Legal, Anthropological and Religious Considerations. New York: The Julian Press Inc.

Roe v. Wade, 410 U. S. 113 (1973).

Swomley, J. M. (1997). Abortion and Public Policy. *Journal of Christian Ethics.* Issue 013, Vol 3, No. 5, December 1997.

United State v Vuitch, 402 U. S. 62 (1971) Vestal, Christine. (2006) States probe limits of abortion policy. Stateline.org.

Webster v. Reproductive Health Services, 492 U. S. 490, (1989) Whelan, III, E. M. 2005. Senate Testimony on *Roe v Wade.*

Wood, Kathryn. Past President, Republican Women of Alabama (1980). Advocate and Lobbyist for Women's Issues, Outreach Coordinator, Counselor, SHE Center and Women's Community Health Center, 1983-2006. Personal conservation, April 10, 2007, Huntsville, AL.

Women's Medical Professional Corp. v Voinovich, 130 F. 3d 187, 209 (6th Cir. 1997).

Women's Rights on Trial, 1st Ed., Gale, 1997, p. 312.

Appendix

Personal Conversation with Kathy

Kathy was given the proposed outline for this public policy paper and asked to address the issues within the outline, or anything she felt like talking about as a person who has worked on the front lines in the abortion field from 1983 to 2006. She is nationally recognized as an advocate for women's rights. Some of the names in this paper are not widely known because of the violence associated with clinic workers especially during the time when there was a Nuremberg list promoting violence...names and location were available on this website to those who wished to perpetuate violence on these individuals calling for the elimination of these "murderers." Kathy was assaulted by a Catholic Priest in the clinic in Huntsville, Alabama and suffered a broken neck. In the end, we found that this outline did not work in addressing the issues as they truly were. Therefore, she wrote a response... in her own voice...her thoughts...unedited.

I conducted this interview to try to place in context what Roe v Wade meant to those who worked in the field. Do they understand what happened? Do any of us understand?

Linda:

I went through the transcript and again decided that this was just an unworkable platform within which to draft a paper. The more I thought about this and the more I looked at this outline the more enraged I became. Policy papers set within these guidelines do nothing to address the core problem. They are part of the problem. Everyone who has done anything knows that if you have the right name behind the study and use statistics etc. you can develop a scope to fit exactly what you want or have been paid to do. Other than this ($$$) what has really been accomplished?

Kathy

I have spent the last few days really going through my memories some of which caused me countless hours of sleep and peace. Because of regulations I could not follow-up on these women. I often wonder if they were able to grasp a glimpse of personal freedom or did, they become beaten down by circumstances. What happened to them – could I have done more – where was the beneficial society – did I waste my life?

The Roe v Wade Supreme Court decision was, in my opinion, a beginning and an end to determination of family and personhood. All eyes were focused on the fetus as a person but without status (IRS does not allow tax deductions for a pregnancy). It set state against state, religious groups against each other, it set up a class system – those who could afford care and those who couldn't, it set up a business climate which, of course, the government could regulate, it set up a pattern of violence and hate, it ushered in a myriad of problems because the ruling never addressed personhood of man, woman, child; responsibility in the context of family, government and society as a whole; equality of health care services.

After 1973, private individuals formed businesses to provide services to more of the population base and an open market. I went to work for Paul Leight in 1983 who had both an abortion clinic and a non-profit birth control segment. I saw the pitfalls and the natural greed in this approach, but that did not lessen my innate feeling that we were not addressing the real problem. Naturally, the government rushed in to get its piece and more court decisions followed which were still not addressing the issue of personhood and/or responsibility. All the actions were punitive to the woman and her decision to maintain her life and family in her own context. All court actions had a religious fervor – guilt, shame, not a good physician, immoral woman, protection of a teenager, rights of the father/ spouse (note it is always a woman/not him that has sinned). The result was a band-aid approach to a specific area to appeal to the wishes of the loudest voices.

It could never address specific instances because each pregnancy presents its own circumstances, we do not live in a world that treats all as the same. In the over 30 years (high school debates and papers in the mid 1960's- activism in the seventy's, eighty's, ninety's, etc.) I have listened to thousands of women pour out their hearts describing their particular circumstances trying to make intelligent decisions. Facing an unwanted pregnancy was a heart wrenching experience and if given the time and a nonjudgmental openness, each woman made her own decision. To examine each woman's plight fully cannot be done in a 15-minute office call, under insurance guidelines, under governmental regulations, under religious/moral overtones, under harassment, under expectations of others. Of all those women I can only remember about thirty who callously disregarded personal responsibility and looked upon abortion as a "right," but they also were the ones that disregarded responsibility for contraception, self, society.

Even the Women's Movement dropped the ball! Women who felt that it was their place to stay in the home and raise their families were made to feel that their contribution to society was worthless. The Government then addressed the loudest voices and put in place special work situations just for women ignoring men. Many women reacted to all of this and tried to become "Super Women" juggling both job and family. Children now were being ignored and were often thought of as a burden which placed a larger burden on the school system, the healthcare system, prison system. You name it, everything and everyone was affected either primarily or secondarily.

The Government again stepped in and through its actions or inactions caused a lessening of research in women's and children's healthcare. The schools were faced with tons of restrictions and in many cases unreasonable goals for education. Psychological avenues and support were closed off to people/families. Religious fervor made many feels as though they were guilty, they alone were bad because they were not like everyone else, if they followed this route all the problems would be solved, and they would not have to be "embarrassed." Always there was the "if you do as I say, you will be taken care of" philosophy.

Again, the band-aid approach. The family is under attack from all angles. People begin to give up – it is all too much for them to handle and most people want to take the easy way out. The Government will take care of me – I do not have to worry about my personal responsibility to self and family, I can always find some group to absolve me of responsibility, I do not have to live "my" life. Societal mores are not important – it is OK to have a child under any circumstances without regard to ramifications to society, the child, self.

From earliest times, women managed their homes. It was their job to find the best mate, have the best family, and establish a place in society which naturally relegated men to the economic provider. In 1859 the AMA began to form using the case that university doctors were much better than practically trained. Education now became a priority for the total population instead of just the wealthy. In the mid 1800's we had a Civil War, a dramatic change in the population demographics, societal upheaval, and economic chaos.

Women took care of medical problems and had an extremely strong network of physicians, midwives, other women to help with whatever they felt they could handle. Yes, it was (and is) a rough road. Privately things were handled. Wealthy women in New England found and used Madame Restell (aka Anna Lohman) to provide discrete abortions. In the Mid-west, West and South, women used the mail order services of Lydia Pinkham to regulate their most private medical emergencies. Margaret Sanger rose in the early1900's to give voice to the inadequate health care of poor women, especially in the slums. I would be willing to bet that these women knew the risks and yet took advantage of what was available because they had the autonomy of self.

In college in the mid sixty's, I knew about the "Jane's." Should one get pregnant, one had only to make it to Minneapolis or Chicago with the right connection number (underground from other women). We knew that although the law stated that contraception was only for married women (Griswold) that we could go to Planned Parenthood with a wedding ring on our finger and get the contraception and in most cases the sex education on birth control, STD's, etc. that we needed and desired without intervention of family, religion, legal constraints. We knew where to go for an abortion if that was our desire. We knew what it was to face private decisions on our own facing whatever consequences that came.

Then times changed and women took a more forceful role in economics which upset the balance and began to redefine social mores. Without a strict structure, things began to fall apart socially giving rise to guilt, inaction, over- reaction, and restrictions – all band-aids with no overall plan. People began to rely on the false premise that someone or something would always provide a safety net – how could they be held responsible for their actions – it was so much easier to put blame on someone or something else. It is so much easier to do what one was told was right than to investigate oneself. A television, 30-minute response to a lifelong situation.

The framework of Roe v Wade also gave rise to groups who felt contraception was also a form of abortion. Restrictions were made on companies – research and availability were affected; companies and choices became limited. Again, the losers were women primarily, men, children, society secondarily. People tried to balance their private lives within a structure over which they had no control. Agencies and "think groups" took control with their statistical studies and projections. Put everyone and every situation into a box – it is easier to understand, graph and develop programs/responses. But no one was listening to the voices of those at the very center of the problems - the core.

Now we get to the point that taxpayers begin to feel that they are being taken advantage of through the Public Health system. Can't these people understand that having children is a larger responsibility than a monthly check? Why can't they use birth control? Why should I take care of (their children…Linda's substitution)? Again, we are expecting all people to think exactly alike. Funds and education are cut. Religious groups feel the need to get involved – we must march lock step with the WORLD – unfortunately, the world has never truly been felt by the disadvantage and - "The poor will be with you always" – so unless they follow our way (we) should be rid of them or made guilty. Even a small mind like mine realizes that my hopes, dreams, concerns, and problems are mine alone and cannot be addressed in a paper or study.

Roe v Wade expressed a framework within legal, moral, and religious studies. It expressed a desire to allow women and men to work within a framework of accepted knowledge to address their situation. It respected the right of individual choice. It should not have been expected to solve the problem.

I do not believe that the Supreme Court believed that those few words would have such an impact on the society. They were talking about freedom to choose within one's own family the destiny of that cell. Then they were faced by all these other issues usually by groups/factions without a "vested" self-interest. Then it became regulations without consideration of personhood. Another band-aid approach to the loudest voices without a long-range goal. I believe in a truly democratic society whether to have an abortion or use contraception would be a totally personal choice without governmental or religious overtones. I believe in the strength of self and concern for others. I believe in the potential for life and regret that so many diminish this concept.

I regret that society pays lip service to the unborn but does not truly support those "values" by providing adequate health care, education, research, and support for families, etc. I regret that our society wants the 30-minute solution to lifelong problems.

I believe in the strength of the family whatever you chose to make as your family. I believe in education, research, solving hard problems but doubt that any of us has the answers to every facet. I accept that I do not have the answers and hope that I can have compassion for all those who struggle with their own problems and demons without judging their choices. As unique individuals, we are just that UNIQUE. Who died and made me God?

Roe v Wade could have been a hallmark decision had it not been left to the political system. It could have redeemed a healthcare problem of quality medical care. It could have supported an ideal of "Every child a wanted child." It could have addressed the personal choice of an individual or those she wished involved in her decision. It could have addressed basic freedom. Unfortunately, people with small minds used it to further their own goals over basic freedoms.

Roe v Wade was a concept of freedom. What has been done to the concept was an abortion of freedom.

Transcript Of Kathy and Dan Conversation

———

Every time we have a war or an economic disaster, i.e., a depression we have a big rise in anti- abortion legislation.

AMA organized in 1859, they called for the general suppression of abortions even those included before quickening because there was a big fight going on between the doctors and the university-trained doctors. This was a move to push out mid-wives and health providers that the poor had. The campaign was basically that they were being treated by frauds.

Lydia Pinkham question.........that is Restell. Lydia Pinkham and Restell knew each other but Lydia was toward the west and Midwest and Restell got all the rich people because at that time all the rich were in the Northeast. Lydia Pinkham mostly worked with poor women, farming women, who did not have a lot of money.

Linda: Statistics?

Between 1800 and 1900 the number of children born to white women (the only group statistics were on) dropped fifty%....7.04 to 3.56 with the visibility of abortions. Women were demanding to control how many children they had. Popular advertisements carried abortifacients to relieve menstrual obstruction blockage. They were unsafe and ineffective ranging from exercise to soap solutions to mild poisons and physical intrusions in the uterus. Induced abortions in the 19th century were estimated to be one in every four live births.

Linda: Margaret Sanger?

Margaret Sanger was about 1913 and her cause was mostly for poor women in slums. We had child labor. That was another reason not to have abortions because we needed all these kids to work in factories. Margaret Sanger worked for the poor women that were constantly pregnant or their husbands were in dangerous positions, and they became widows stuck trying to raise seven or more kids. They had no idea of hygiene and not practically methods.

Linda: What we are discussing is the background of the problem and the political realities of Madame Restell, Lydia Pinkham, and the Catholic Church.

Kathy: Yes, and other religions because we were faced with the Puritanism ethic; we were also faced with religions that wanted ethnic purity. They were anti catholic, anti-foreigners of all types. We were dealing with a full range of religious hypocrisy and that bled over into our political and legal system.

Linda: So along with those political realities we had eco- nomic realities and those had to do with females who were wealthy and females who were poor. We divide those between Restell and Pinkham. To tie in the social implications along with political and eco- nomic in the background that would pertain to.........

Kathy: Restell because her clients were never attacked. She was later attacked and arrested but nothing was ever proven. Lydia Pinkham got away with it because she was doing a general mail order business and she sold all kinds of things. Her products that were abortifacients were not just sold as this but as vitamins...all kinds of things.... she had good marketing skills. She had things like juniper berries to make your own contraceptives.... you cooked them and stewed them...and made a black paste and you ate that

Linda: What did it do?

Kathy: I do not know. It is like yams. Black women, a lot of them used yams as contraceptives because they have an extremely elevated level of estrogen which prevented the sperms from moving. Aboriginal people in Australia use yams.

Linda: To this day....

Kathy: Uh huh.......it is not always effective, but it works. All you need to do is to miss one pregnancy a year

Linda: Page 35 in this book Tribe Key Actors?

Kathy: Restell, Pinkham and Sanger Tribe goes a lot into statistics with maps......concentrating on the U. S.

Linda: Roe v Wade had to go into background leading to Roe v Wade......so what we covered were the key actors leading up to the policy but not the policy itself so the key actors would be Roe, the Texas lawmakers and the Supreme Court Justices.......

Kathy: Betty Friedman, the rise of the feminist movement in the early sixty's.... college enrollment for women increased 57 percent, women working outside the homes doubled and were not allowed to have jobs if they were pregnant......fertility dropped; there was disparity between men and women's treatment in the workplace.... contraceptives started to become available....

Linda: That may be critiquing what happened after the policy was implemented but the political leaders would be those people who brought the case and the Supreme Court Justices with the primary stakeholders being the women and families affected by abortion

Linda: We are at Stakeholders?

Kathy: Stakeholders would be women of all classes, the men they are involved with (secondary); the children (secondary) although basically what our laws have done is to put children into a category where they are not important. We have disenfranchised thou-sand and thousands of children by forcing pregnancy. They are unwanted; they cannot be adopted; we do not have hospitals for them; we do not have schools for them; we do not have food for them; or clothing (water?) ...yes...we have ruined our future by forcing women, families, whatever their family is made of.... we forced them into a situation through our laws...through our moral hypocrisy that we have predestined the demise of our society.

Linda: So, the target publics would be society at large

Kathy: Yes. That is the way I see this whole thing. When you have children that have no one to care for them... physically, emotionally, socially.... these children are growing up. We are having to build more prisons, more special schools...we are forcing our children into non-educable situations because they are just reacting from anger, rather than where they could be an asset.

Linda: And this is because the mother is

Kathy: Mother is.... if she is forced to carry a pregnancy by a governmental law...if she unable to have contraception so she can control reproduction.... if programs are not available to help her know how to raise a child because she in many instances has come from a dysfunctional family. We have got the child abuse thing...anger...all kinds of health care problems...they are all coming back to the fact that women know what is right for themselves. If supported to prevent pregnancy, or know what the restrictions are, or understand how much it takes to deal with a child maybe we could cut down a whole bunch of problems. We do not have sex education any- more...

Linda: We have abstinence only.......

Kathy: That is right. That does not help. Telling kids to just say no has never worked because we can go back through history thousands of years and see it does not work.

Linda: So, in looking at the background to all of this, once again recapping the political, social, and economic implications how could you sum all that up?

Kathy: There is no easy answer to any of this. What we are stuck with is all the ramifications of what I present policy...social disorder, educational dis- order. We have restrictive laws; we are disregarding rights of women, men and especially children. We are trying to force moral values on other countries of the world, which may or may not have our value or our means. We have ruined...successfully ruined many of the companies providing birth control, birth control information, and healthcare. We have stunted the educational process by removing sex education replacing it with abstinence only. We have stunted education in that we have children not cared for in schools where they cannot be handled. We do not have hospitals to handle children who are born of drug addicted parents because our society has collapsed.

Linda: O.K. Let us look then at the Program Development. The program that emerged from Roe v. Wade...the eligibility, the nature of the Rules and Regulations, the expected outcomes, fiscal support... What I tried to do was to say that they did not put forth a program. It was sent back to the States to develop Rules and Regulations. Those who were eligible at first were the women over eighteen and then they went back and in 1976 said O.K. girls who are eighteen are younger can have an abortion if one parent approves or they have a judicial bypass. Some of this came about in 1977. The expected out- comes, I just said I did not know what they expected the outcome of all this to be. There was really no money. Medicaid only paid for services if it threatened the life of the mother or if there were fetal abnormalities

Kathy: Now prior to 1976, Medicaid paid for abortions for Medicaid patients. That was one of the ways that the antis went after it. They said their tax dollars should not be used to pay for what they classified as murder; however, there was not the opposite point of view of people saying well my tax dollars to be used to force women to have pregnancies. That has been a real split...that was a big split in the women's movement because they said that any woman who desired to have a child should be allowed to have a child whether she had support or not. Now a lot of taxpayers do not agree with this.

Linda: Would I be correct in saying that the programs that emerged came not from the Supreme Court?

Kathy: They just gave an outline. First 12 weeks no harassment; second 12 weeks the states were allowed some say, and they really restricted it in the third trimester.

Linda: So, what did they expect to gain from this? What were the expected outcomes?

Kathy: it was just a placating. I have Weddington's book here. I don't know if she goes into it...it was just a hot potato at the time, and they were looking to flip it up because that was...when Roe v Wade came down that was '73...the feminist movement was really pressing hard. The government was it with all kinds of labor relations. You could not fire a woman for being pregnant; you had to start paying them better. It has been the trade-off affect. We will placate these people, and they will not let us see what is going on over here. Business for this will hide it. That is why I see the Supreme Court decision throwing it back to the states and let the states deal with it.

Linda: So, the implementation phase was tough because not all states implemented alike.

Kathy: Right. We have fifty different laws, and it has gotten more convoluted as it has gone on because we have added different things.

Linda: I do not know then, how one could say whether the program was successfully implemented or not because of the political and economic climate but more so the political climate would have kept it from being implemented. Would that be correct?

Kathy: I would say so.

Linda: There was no budget for it at all?

No there never has been a budget for family planning. If you look at our health services, our county health services and such, the first thing that is cut is sexually transmitted diseases unless it is syphilis or gonorrhea is starting to get a little more important...Chlamydia...those are cut... birth control...cut...because we are back to the abstinence phase.

Linda: Do you think you could talk about skilled service providers because they are becoming fewer? In the beginning were the service providers' skilled back in the seventy's or were they all learning?

Kathy: there were a few that were skilled. In Huntsville we saw people like Dr. Drake who trained through the medical school and trained many of the gynecologists in Alabama and family practice physicians on how to do abortions at the clinic.

Linda: Dr. Drake was an African American?

Kathy: Yes...who was run over....

Linda: Do you think it was politically motivated that he was run over?

Kathy: It is a good chance. It has never been solved. It was a hit and run.

Linda: On his bicycle...as I recall.

LINDA ROBERTSON BOURGEOIS, PH.D.

Kathy: Um-hum.

Linda: So, he trained here in Alabama and so I would assume that other states would have people who would go in and train...

Kathy: Right. He also spent a lot of time.... we also had mid-wives at that time, especially in the poorer parts of the county and he trained them and would be their back up if they got into trouble. Many babies were born at home or at a maternity house where you went just to deliver.

Linda: What about hospitals? Did they provide any serv ices for abortions?

Kathy: No, not really. Presently, no. You could not get anybody to do an open abortion in a hospital because of the political and religious climate and economic. Insurance companies do not pay for it, and you sure do not want your fellow church members to find out that you performed one or even your partners...your medical partners because of the pressure. Yes, there are some very well-trained physicians in this country. Some of them extremely specialized like the Wichita Clinic and the one in Colorado. Atlanta has some fantastic doctors, but they are so far and few between. The level of care providers for abortions and contraceptive services for medium to poor income women especially with no insurance have fallen off...I do not remember the percentages...but they are not available in most of the counties, i.e., 83 percent...in this country do not have care services.

Linda: Going into the evaluation of what happened. I think the background and evaluation of what happened are the two most important things in my mind. Did the program fail? Did they do the wrong thing, or did they do the right thing wrongly?

Kathy: it personally failed miserably because at one time there was a protected status of the family. Did not matter what level your family was, but the family was able to take care of itself and make decisions for itself.

By doing this we have stripped it away. It is o.k. to father 6 or 7 kids with 5 or 6 women...it is o.k. We now have children at 12 and 13 believing it is the right thing to do. You are an adult if you get pregnant or if you get someone pregnant. We have taken away that family restriction on how to grow up; how to care about other people...it is all self, and the government will take care of us.

Linda: Do you think this grew out of Roe v. Wade?

Kathy: I think part of it did. I really do because once the restrictions came on and we had the rise of women's rights and things we had (Dan came in) ...I think when they said that states had responsibilities, they ruined that you decide what is going in your life. They took away the personhood of women; they took away the structure that we had to work with; and they said the state can make the decision. That was the beginning.

Linda: Do you think we should keep Roe v. Wade?

Kathy: the issue is always going to be with us. Roe v. Wade is not an effective law, and it probably should be repealed. But I also think that something real must take its place. This issue is not an issue for the government; for religion; this is a private personal issue and should not be.... its...I do not believe that government has any right in deciding whether someone has a child or not. Can you think of a better law to replace it?

I do not think you can write an effective law to cover something so private and personal. I do believe they must if they are going to continue this path relying on the framework of Roe v. Wade, the government must provide adequate education.... sexual responsibility to self and others...respecting diversity. We have got to get the religious overtones out of the language. We have got to make it safe for doctors and health practitioners and hospitals to provide the care that is appropriate to the choice of the woman and those she chooses to include in this especially crucial decision.

Linda: You could see it being folded into a healthcare bill?

Kathy: Yes. Absolutely and I think when we do that, we are also going to have the thing with part of the population saying, "Well I don't my tax money go for contraception or abortion." We have also got to consider the other people out there saying "I don't want my tax dollars forcing women to have children they don't want."

Linda: And there are people who do not want to see their tax dollars used to raise kids.

Kathy: Right or to provide for foster care services and abuse care services. This whole health care thing is where it must be addressed but we got so many pieces to it because we are so fragmented now that I do not think there can ever be a cohesive bill to address all the problems that have been set up by our hypocrisy.

Pause............Just talking......... Kathy,

I am not sure that any of the following should be included. What do you think? The color/culture statement but we seemed to have wandered off the Roe v. Wade issue.

You had the men going off to work in the Northern cities and the women stayed home while they bred at home and dad came home and he was not going to take responsibility for some other dude's kid. They became a very matriarchal society...women took care of everything. Well, it did not work.

Linda: With the Hispanics? Go back over that again? Dan enters the room and offers this.......

Kathy: Everybody always acts like color is the big problem.... I have always said that color is not the problem culture is. Until they decide to adopt and integrate into Western Civilizations, so to speak, then they are never going to succeed.

Linda: I am so glad I have you on tape.... please continue.

Kathy......but that is basically it.

Linda: Its culture?

Kathy...culture is a huge problem in all this. It affects economics ...

Dan...like I told Mike...he came back from UNA and was talking about discrimination and all that.... I said ******** do not give me all that. These people have been here for a hundred years and free and in a hundred years they have not made any progress. The Japanese have completely integrated into our society, and we fought a world war with them...30 years ago...they got the work ethic, and their values are the same as Western Europe.

Linda: It is the Hispanics who are going to become the majority in America according to the Census Bureau prediction.

Kathy.... They are the ones that are striving; they are pushing. Now interestingly enough if you listen to enough of the right-wing channels there is a DVD out to teach Hispanics illegal, how to become members of the society and get through all the red tape and everything. They are against it. I am saying...this is stupid. We need a society that has working people with goals.

Dan......I do not think they should be allowed into the country illegally......

Kathy... No but if they are here...

Dan...they should make a concerted effort to stop illegal immigration but at the same time there is not a problem with them going through the same process as others going through the immigration process...

Kathy.... right

Dan......another problem is why in the ***** do we have multilingual ballots and signs and all this other ****. That should never be mandated by law.

Kathy.... No

Dan...If a business wants to do it, fine. It is on their nickel and increasing their business opportunities, but the government should never do it.

Linda: Is it called for in the Constitution?

Dan.... No. English is the language of this country just like Japanese is in Japan just like Spanish is in Spain.

Kathy.... well, you cannot put a child in Mexico unless they are lingual in their language. You cannot.

Dan.... It makes no sense to the ******* political parties....it does not matter what the argument is they are not going to be on the same side. It is like two three-year-old...r2; am not; r2; am not.... They are ******* idiots. They do not use any common sense.

Linda: I am going to have to bleep you out!

Kathy......well all our legislation, in probably the last 30 years, has been a band aide approach to a problem. Whoever screams the loudest that gets taken care of and it covers over what the real problems are.

Start back here, maybe?

Linda: Is that what the religious people did with Roe v Wade?

Kathy: Yes. Everybody now wants the problem solved within 30 minutes. Your marriage problems are solved in 30 minutes...one visit to a counselor... that is enough...your mental health issues...just give you some pills, you will go away...

Dan...the television generation.

Kathy...yes, everything is what I want...there is nobody looking at a broad picture. Our society is so scrambled up and nobody has a broad view. Our politicians do not. You cannot even get churches to agree on anything. You cannot get schools, teachers, to agree on anything. Everybody has their own little pet way of solving the problem. I like the one comment in the Christian Ethics article...when we eat an egg, we do not say it is a chicken. We do need to point out that whereas life is important this is only a potential for a life is always there. It can be taken or given either naturally or unnaturally. We have potential when we are born under the Constitution. We are not created equally; we have a potential for an equal. It is up to us to arrive at what that is to the best of our level, but we do not have the services for it.

Linda: Where to go from here......

Kathy: they tried to do the right thing but did it wrongly.

Linda: What do you mean by that?

Kathy: Meaning that when Roe v Wade got passed it just set up a framework for more dissension. It also set up little pet theories or whatever. It fueled the feminist movement; it fueled the religious right; it did not help the medical...the social and medical system at all because there was no support there. That was the first wrong thing. The feminist movement in many ways hurt our society because they barged in demanding things without looking or respecting women of opposite views; women who wanted to stay home; women who wanted families were not given the same respect. They were looked down upon which is our society in general. We are always looking down on or trying to keep somebody down. Maybe that is human nature, but we did not concentrate on the needs and work with them and develop them fully into a comprehensive pro- gram. That is what we did wrongly. We took away things but did not replace them.

Linda: Looking at outline....... I thought I would write the background, what went on before and leading up to Roe v. Wade because that is an important part of Roe v. Wade and why we have the policy. This may be the most important. Then we had Roe v. Wade which brought about so much discontent and violence which has not even been addressed. So, during the implementation phase of Roe v Wade, we had a lot of violence, and I do not know how that played into policy. Once you get the background to the policy there is not much left to write about except a little bit about what the states did; there were thirty laws (cases decided) after Roe v. Wade...but the important thing with the policy is that it brought about violence. Even though it provided services for women, the impact of it was that it impacted the society in such a way that people were killed; they were abused by the language of the religious right...

They had services taken away

Linda: Yes, services were taken away.

Kathy: And became more limited after Roe v. Wade in many respects. Contraception was limited; sex education was limited...

Linda: There is no way to evaluate the policy without evaluating all fifty states.

Kathy: And there is no way to evaluate the policy because you cannot compare the laws of fifty states to the federal policy and to what the federal health care system is....

Linda: It is not part of the health care system. It is an arm separate...even though it is within the Public Health Department...under that umbrella...and all the states are under that umbrella of the Public Health Department but there is no money there except for Inspectors who come and inspect and for people who write the Rules and Regulations. There is absolutely no other money there for services except in the Medicaid program which comes under yet a different arm of the Public Health Department. Then when you think about the services provided, they are provided by independent clinics not public service clinics. There is a dichotomy here that you cannot mesh.

Kathy: Right. That is the biggest failure.

Linda: That is the biggest failure because they separated the services from the public.

Kathy: that is the biggest problem. We have set up restrictive laws on private enterprise without protections that are available to other businesses. We have allowed a political cli- mate that also restricts free enterprise. We got nothing! The amazing thing is if you go back and read all this stuff, no number of laws, court cases, from parental notification to spousal notification to whether you are first trimester, second trimester or what is going to make a difference. There is always going to be abortions of some kind. What we need to do is to make sure that there are fewer and concentrate more on sup- porting the people involved in making the right decision considering and respecting other people.

Linda: Stakeholders.

We are all political leaders; we are all primary stakeholders; we are all secondary stakeholders. The whole society is involved. There are no real key actors. What we are now trying to look at is trying to examine how to repair the problem. Potential wins...none. Losses at stake...our whole society. There has never been any program development. We have only had a band aid approach. Program service/treatment; eligibility of service...

Linda: The only thing I talked about there was when they had to go back and make provisions for those under the age of eighteen because as we well know incest begins incredibly early.

Kathy: Expected outcomes.... there could not have been any. Feds threw it out to the states and the states have never funded it. There has been no fiscal support. Impact on implementation...if you did not have implementation... there was not anything. The expected between program functions and program budgets are important...there was not any. You just make that statement.... There was no implementation. So, it cannot be evaluated. You cannot describe something that was not implemented. When you get to evaluation, because of the non-implementation, the negatives are......the positives that could be realized with implementation are....

Linda: That is where I need help.... I do not know what the "Are's" are anymore. I would have to stop and think. I get lost.

Kathy: You are not going to get many class discussions on this issue....

Linda: After recorder turned off some comments made. I took notes.

Kathy: Because of the non-implementation and non-funding society is now faced with the realities of that crisis of non-action. It was mandated by the Supreme Court. There was no fiscal support only reactions to various social groups.... actions were taken to solidify funding in a Band Aid approach. Social and religious factions wanted to preserve their society without any action to strengthen healthcare. This became punitive to the person without addressing medical realities. Society cares more about the fetus than the woman. Poor women have been impregnated by rich men who cannot have this known because it would come down on the man's family. Reference to the movie segment –

Monty Python – "Meaning of Life" - Every Sperm is Sacred. Fetus cannot be deducted because tax laws/codes do not recognize the personhood of a fetus. When you have a scrambled egg for break- fast do you think you are eating a scrambled chicken?

Timeline of significant U. S. Reproductive Rights Events

— 1821 Connecticut passes the first law in the United States barring abortions after "quickening."

— 1873 Congress passes "Comstock Laws," prohibiting sending information and devices for the prevention of conception through the mails, on the grounds that such are "obscene, lewd, lascivious, filthy, indecent and disgusting."

— 1916 Margaret Sanger opens first birth control clinic in the U.S. and goes to jail.

— 1918 New York Court of Appeals empowers legally practicing physicians to prescribe contraceptives for married couples if necessary "to cure or prevent disease."

— 1923 Sanger opens Birth Control Clinical Research Bureau, a clinic dispensing contraceptives under the supervision of a physician.

— 1929 Sanger's clinic is raided, physicians and nurses are arrested, and supplies and records are seized.

— 1936 Sanger challenges the "Comstock Laws" by importing a package of diaphragms. In U.S. v. One Package, the U.S. Circuit Court of Appeals rules that the U.S. Tariff Act of 1930 cannot be construed to forbid the importing of contraceptives for use by physicians in saving lives or promoting well-being.

— 1937 North Carolina becomes the first state to recognize birth control as a public health measure to provide contraceptive services to low-income mothers through its public health pro- grams.

— 1940 Connecticut upholds a state statute that makes use of contraceptives illegal.

— 1942 The Birth Control Federation of America, Inc., changes its name to Planned Parenthood Federation of America, Inc.

— 1960 Food and Drug Administration approves the use of oral contraceptives.

— 1965 U.S. Supreme Court finds unconstitutional the Connecticut law prohibiting birth control for married couples in Griswold v Connecticut.

— 1970 Congress enacts Title X of the Public Health Service Act, providing family planning services, education, and research.

— New York enacts the most liberal abortion law in the nation.

— 1971 Congress repeals most of the provisions of the federal "Comstock Laws."

— 1972 In Eisenstadt v. Baird, the U.S. Supreme Court strikes down a Massachusetts statute that bars distribution of contraceptives to unmarried people.

— 1973 Abortion is legalized nationwide by the

— U.S. Supreme Court's decision in Roe v. Wade. 1976 Congress adopts the first Hyde Amendment barring the use of federal Medicaid funds to provide abortions to poor women. This action marks the beginning of a continuing series of amendments to federal laws to restrict abortion access to various groups of people receiving medical care through the government.

— 1977 The Hyde Amendment is revised to allow states to deny Medicaid funding except in cases of rape, incest, or "severe and long-lasting"" damage to the woman's physical health.

— First reported arson at an abortion clinic, in St. Paul, Minnesota, and first known bombing of an abortion clinic, in Cincinnati, Ohio.

— 1991 In Rust v. Sullivan, the U.S. Supreme Court rules that family planning clinics which receive Title X funding can be forbidden to answer clients' questions about abortion.

— 1992 Planned Parenthood of Southeastern Pennsylvania reaffirms the "core" holdings of Roe v. Wade that women have a right to abortion before fetal viability but allows states to restrict abortion access so long as these restrictions do not impose an "undue burden" on women seeking abortions.

— 1993 Newly inaugurated President Bill Clinton revokes the 1988 Title X "gag rule" and restores the previous policy requiring non-directive options counseling and appropriate referrals.

— Dr. David Gunn is murdered outside of Pensacola Women's Medical Services in Florida.

— 1994 Dr. John Britton, Lt. Col. Jim Barrett, Shannon Lowrey, and Leanne Nichols are murdered in shootings at three abortion clinics.

— In Madsen v Women's Health Center, the U.S. Supreme Court upholds a Florida Supreme Court injunction establishing a "buffer zone" around an abortion clinic to protect access to its entrance.

— 1998 On January 29 a bomb at New Women's Clinic in Birmingham, Alabama, kills an off-duty police officer working as a security guard and critically injures a clinic nurse.

— On October 23, a sniper shoots through a kitchen window and kills Dr. Barnett Slepian in his home in upstate New York.

Sources:

Planned Parenthood Federation of America National Abortion Federation

Timeline Of Abortion Debate

— 1800's: Abortion is legal and common.

— 1900: Abortion is illegal across the United State

— 1965: *Griswold v. Connecticut.* Prohibition of contraceptives by married couples in Connecticut overturned by Supreme Court.

— 1972: *Eisenstadt v. Baird.* Prohibition of birth control to unmarried adults struck down by the Supreme Court.

— 1967-1973: Seventeen states rewrite abortion laws. Four states – Alaska, Hawaii, New York, and Washington – repeal bans entirely.

— 1973: Historic *Roe v. Wade* Supreme Court Decision. The Court by a 7-2 count strikes down a Texas law banning abortion and divides pregnancy into three trimesters; declares that during the first 13 weeks of pregnancy the decision should be left up to "the attending physician, in consultation with his patient".

— 1976: *Planned Parenthood of Central Missouri v. Danforth.* A requirement for parents and spouses to consent to an abortion is struck down by the Supreme Court.

— 1980: *Harris v. McRae.* Supreme Court upholds the Hyde amendment which restricts Medicaid funding of abortions to those procedures needed to protect the life of the pregnant woman and to those required in other exceptional circumstances.

— 1983: *Akron v Akron Center for Reproductive Health.* A city ordinance requiring that all abortions after the first trimester be performed at a hospital and that parental consent be required for abortions on girls under fifteen is invalidated by Supreme Court.

— 1986: *Thornburgh v. American College of Obstetricians & Gynecologists.* Pennsylvania statue requiring a woman seeking an abortion to receive a state-sponsored lecture from her doctor about potential risks and detailing alternatives are struck down by the Supreme Court.

— 1989: *Webster v. Reproductive Health Services.* Missouri law banning the use of public employees or facilities for abortion and requiring physicians to perform tests to determine viability on fetuses of more than 20 weeks' gestation upheld by the Supreme Court.

— 1992: *Planned Parenthood of Southwestern Pennsylvania v. Casey.* Supreme Court abandons trimester plan and adopts a new test – abortion regulations that present an "undue burden" on women's constitutional right will be prohibited. The Casey ruling also upheld the core of *Roe v. Wade* and bans states from outlawing most abortions.

Source:

NPR

Epilogue

This paper written in 2007, met the requirements for a Public Policy class for a doctoral degree. The research is mine; I conducted the personal interview with Kathy and Dan and obtained verbal permission to include this conversation.

I was reared in Mississippi, the first state to legalize abortion in 1966, in cases of rape. I cannot think of a better time to publish than now.

Don't miss out!

Visit the website below and you can sign up to receive emails whenever Linda Robertson Bourgeois, Ph.D. publishes a new book. There's no charge and no obligation.

https://books2read.com/r/B-A-AOAQ-XPGRB

BOOKS 2 READ

Connecting independent readers to independent writers.

Also by Linda Robertson Bourgeois, Ph.D.

Dear Mr. President, Complex Thoughts from the Past, Diversity and
Inclusion
Opening Doors: Roe v Wade

About the Publisher

Dr. Bourgeois is the daughter of Wilton and Gertrude Henning Robertson. Her paternal line is: Wiliam Valentine and Annie Beulah Ross Robertson; Waddy and Susan Patience Meek Ross; Dr. James Meek. My sister and I still lease 77 acres of land of the original 640 acres our great, great grandfather leased for 99 years in 1838. Hence the name...Meek, Ross, Robertson...MRR Publishers.